MW01596360

ISBN-13: 978-0692769669 (FOLDFISH)

ISBN-10: 0692769668

ABOUT THE AUTHOR

Hello,

My name is Pete and I have been an art educator for over twenty years. I began working on this book in the late 1980's. I had gone to a party and somebody made a hat then a boat. He then tore up the paper and made a shirt. I was amazed and it took me a while to reverse engineer the folds. The story just flowed as I practiced telling it.

I later figured out how to make these amazing fish. I combined both in a rough draft by mid 1996. Life happened, and I put the files away as I focused on day to day teaching. I enjoy teaching and I am constantly challenging my students, to get the very best from them. Teaching requires a special type of mind set. Many times, personal projects are put aside, so you can focus on your students needs and goals.

So here I am in 2016. My friends declared it "the year of Pete". They pushed me to "junk" my super rusty car, buzz off my comb-over and get those books published. I believe life is an adventure and when opportunity knocks we need to be prepared. No more excuses allowed. I don't want to be the teacher who doesn't practice what he preaches. So I dug up those old discs, and cleaned up my files. It took all summer but here it is. I hope you enjoy this as much as I have.

So... I dedicate this book:

To my Friends,
Who declared 2016 as my year.

And

To my Students
"Challenge Accepted!"

Congratulations on taking on the **FOLDFISH** challenge. The instructions are laid out as simply as possible, but you will have to problem solve, in order to get them to work. Don't give up, if it doesn't work on the first attempt... Just keep trying. Trust me, it really works well and these fish are a ton of fun.

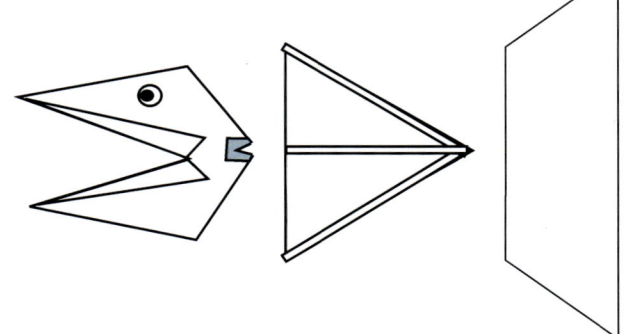

Basic Supplies

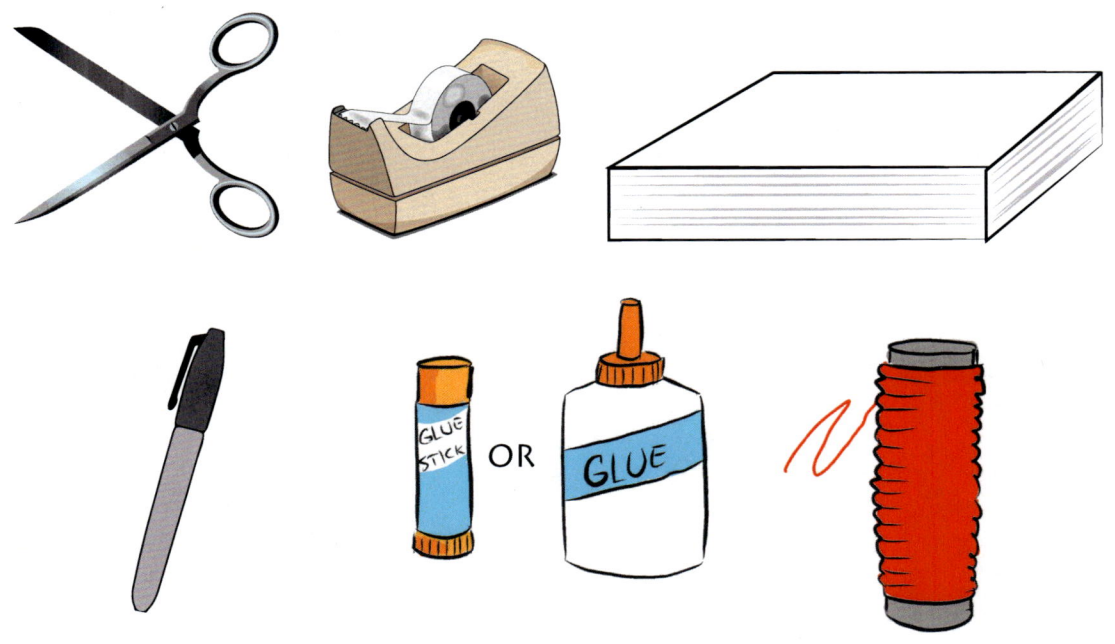

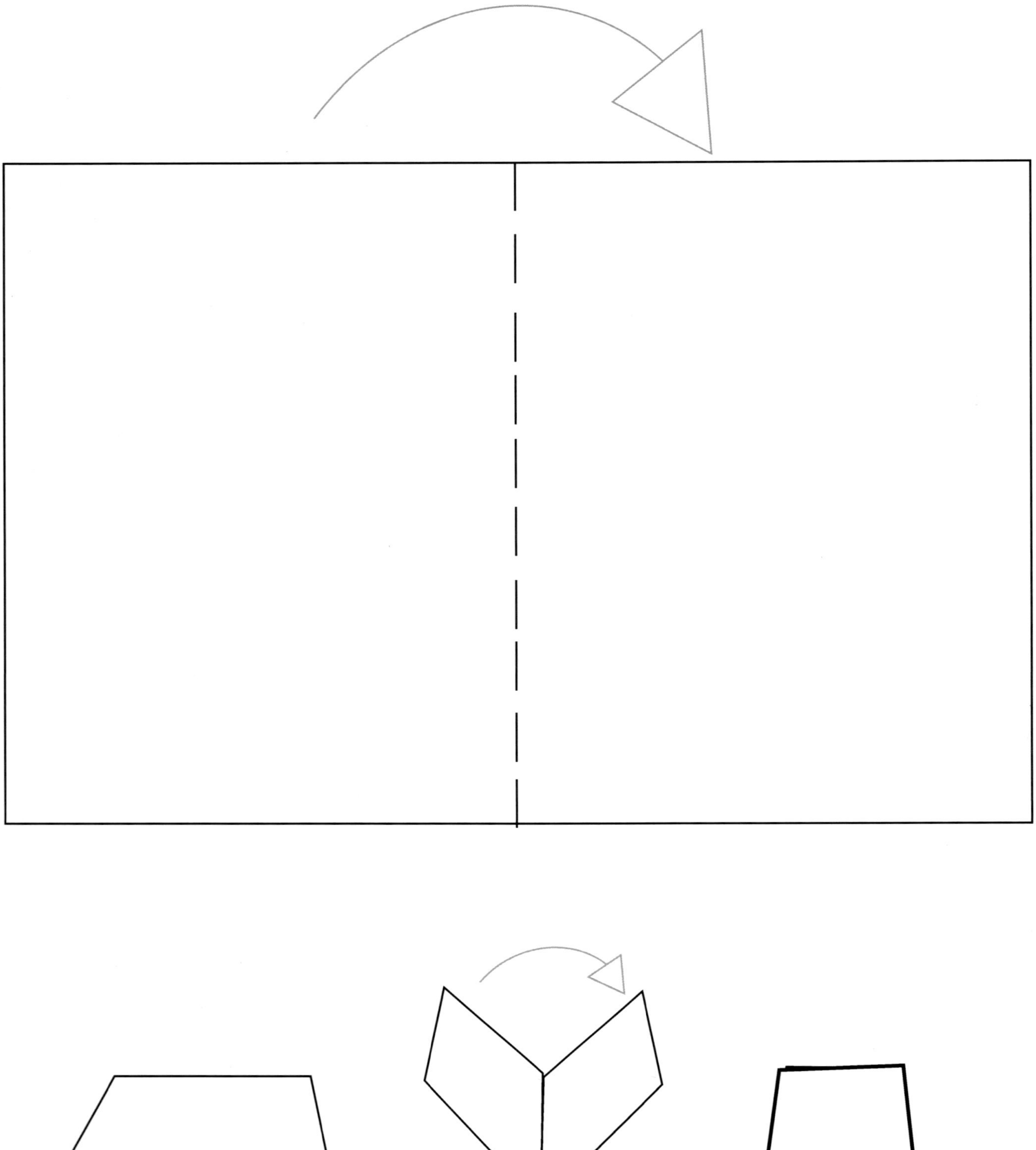

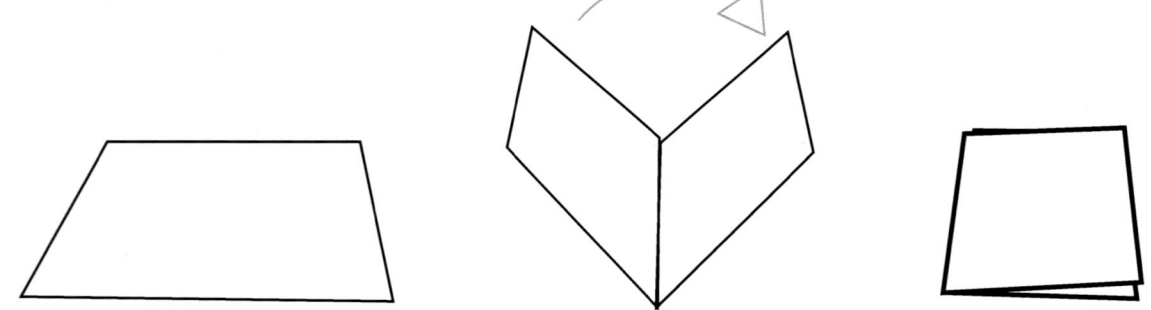

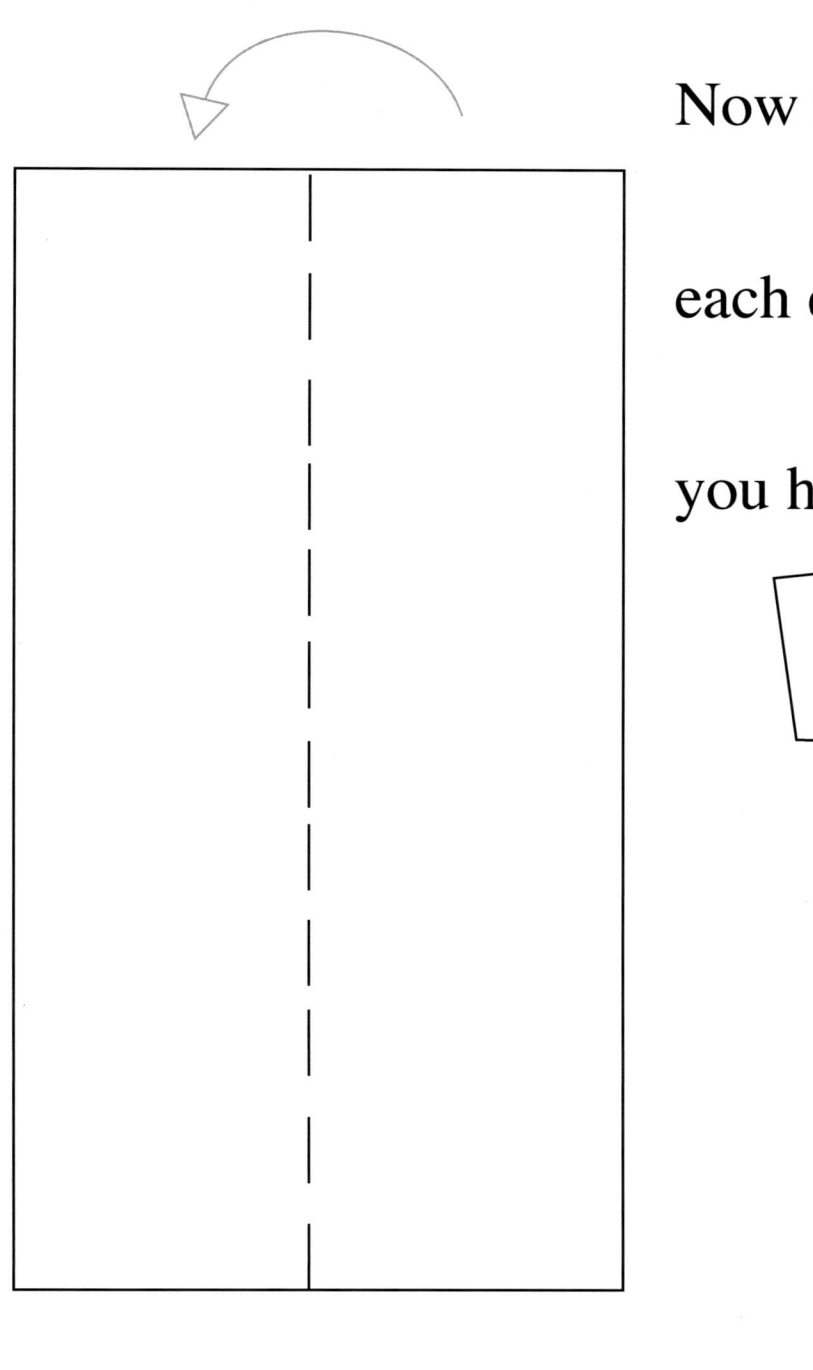

Now fold back

each end until

you have a "W"

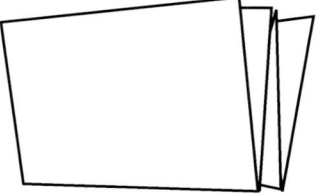

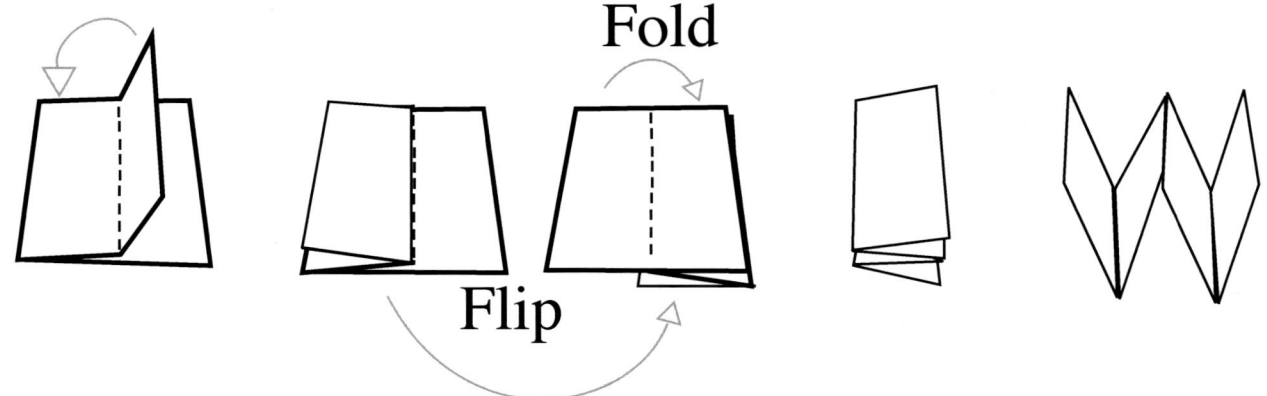

Fold

Flip

Now push down your
"w" so it looks like an
upsidedown "T"

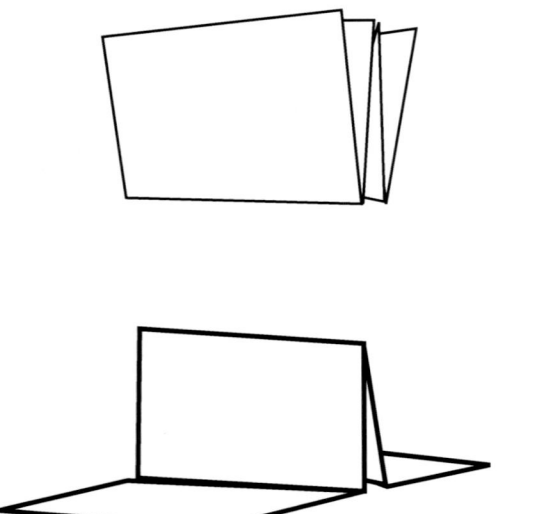

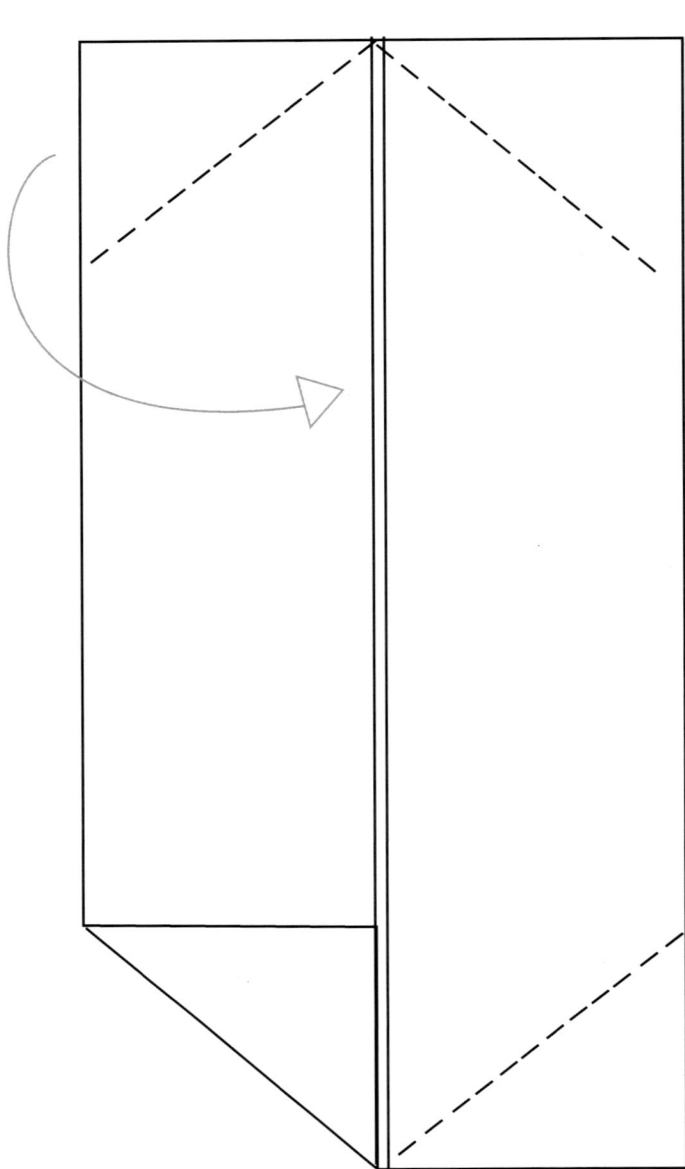

Fold each corner over
to the center crease

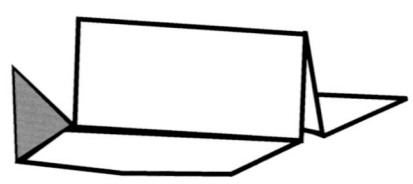

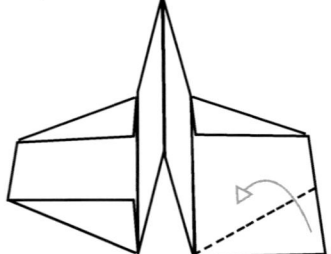

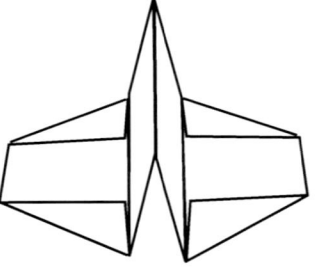

Fold the corners down to the center

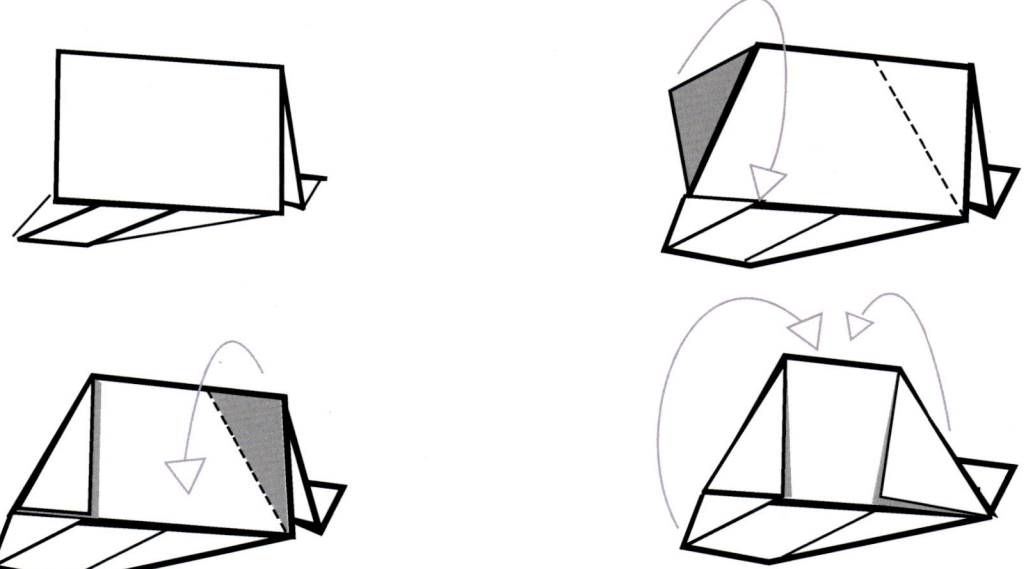

Place the three edges together

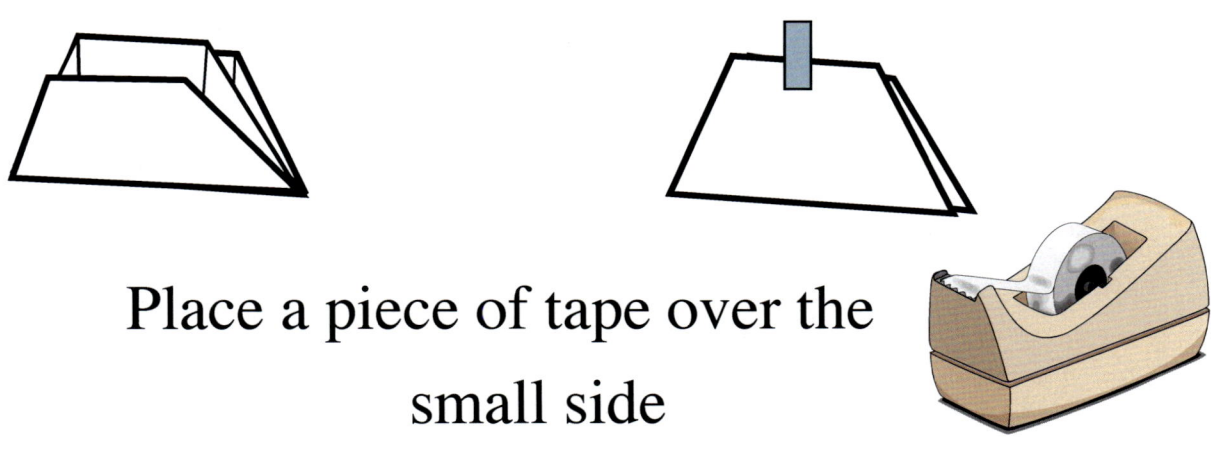

Place a piece of tape over the small side

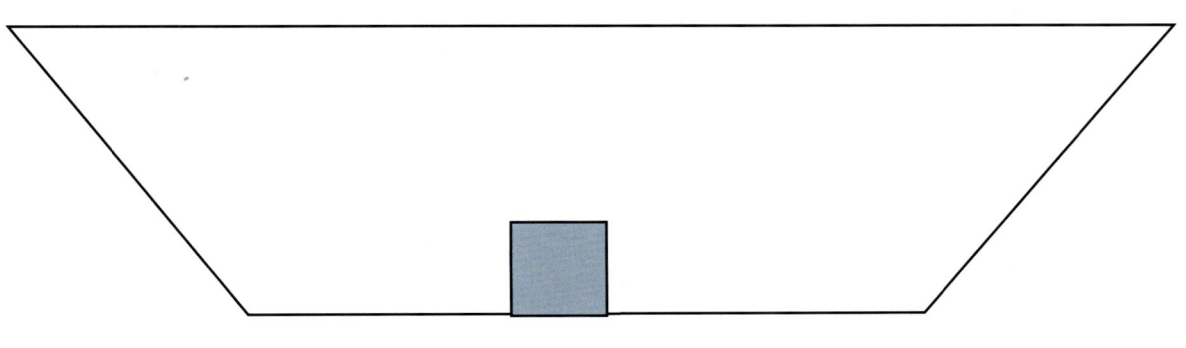

Looks like a taco

Cut a small triangle out of the taped end

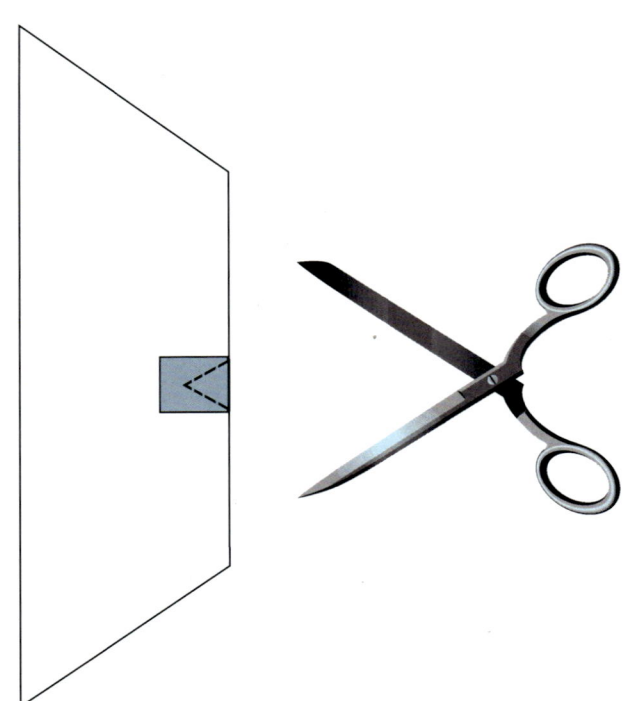

🛑 This is where you STOP when you make the tail

Cut a line about a 1/2 inch

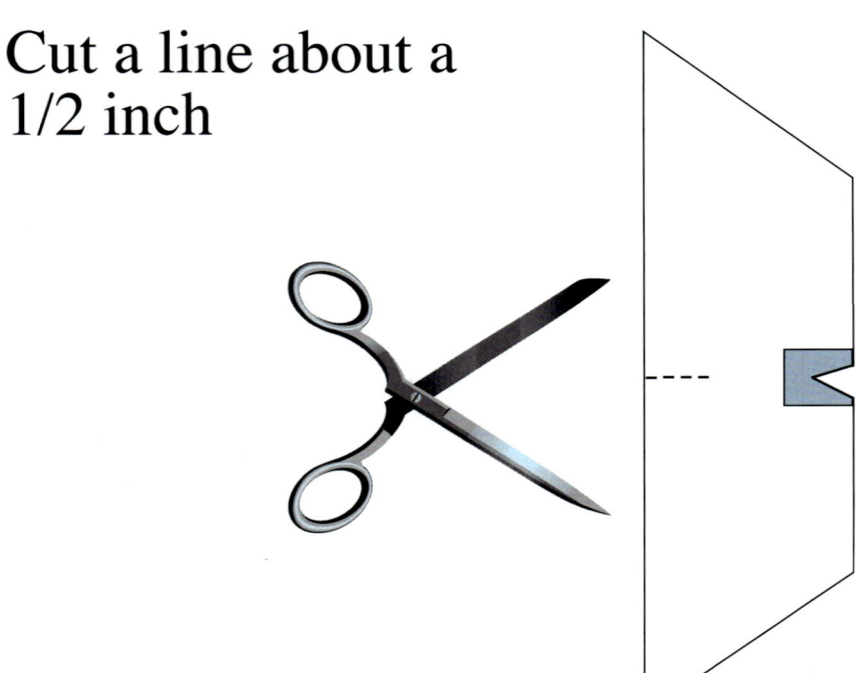

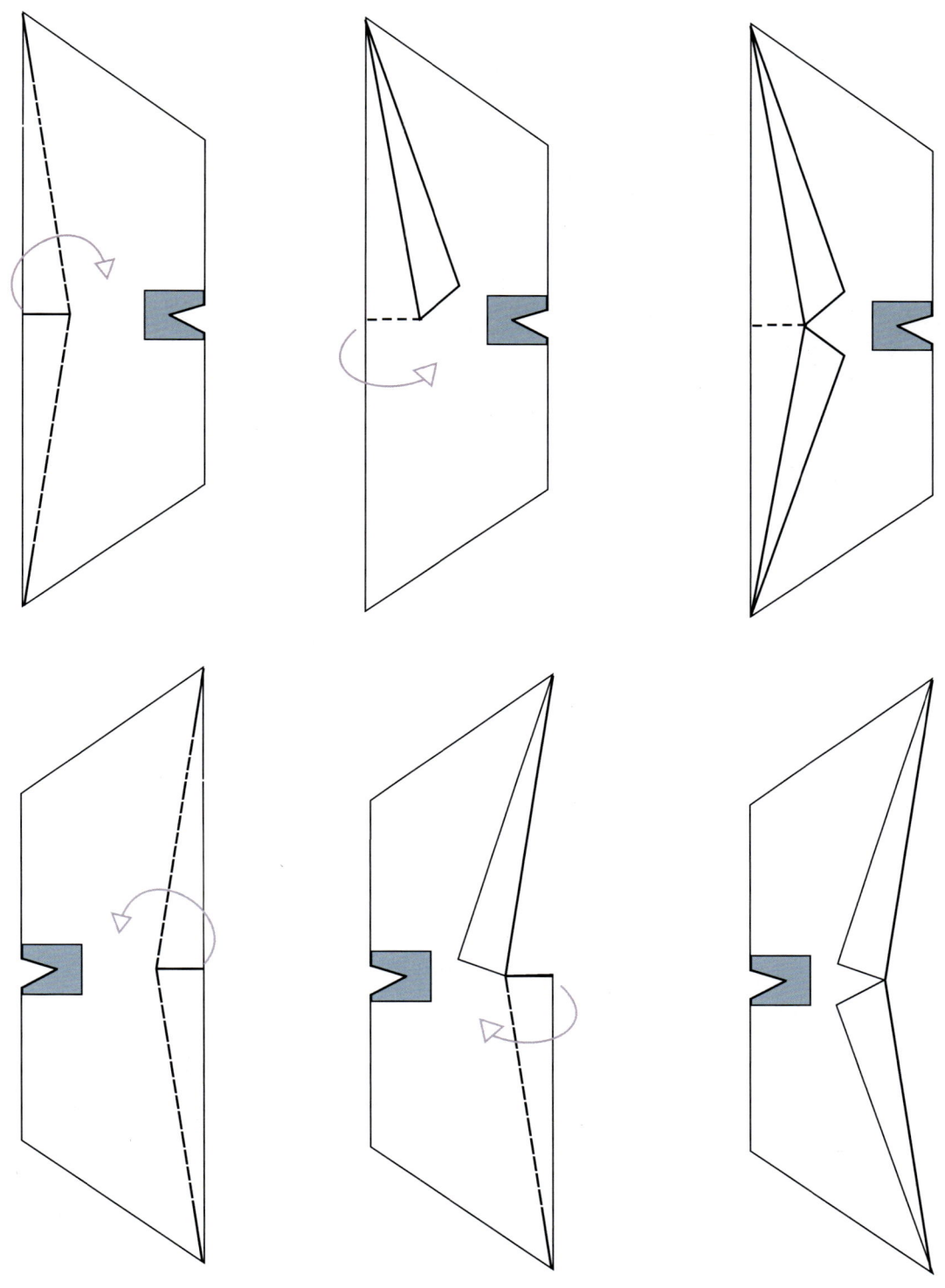

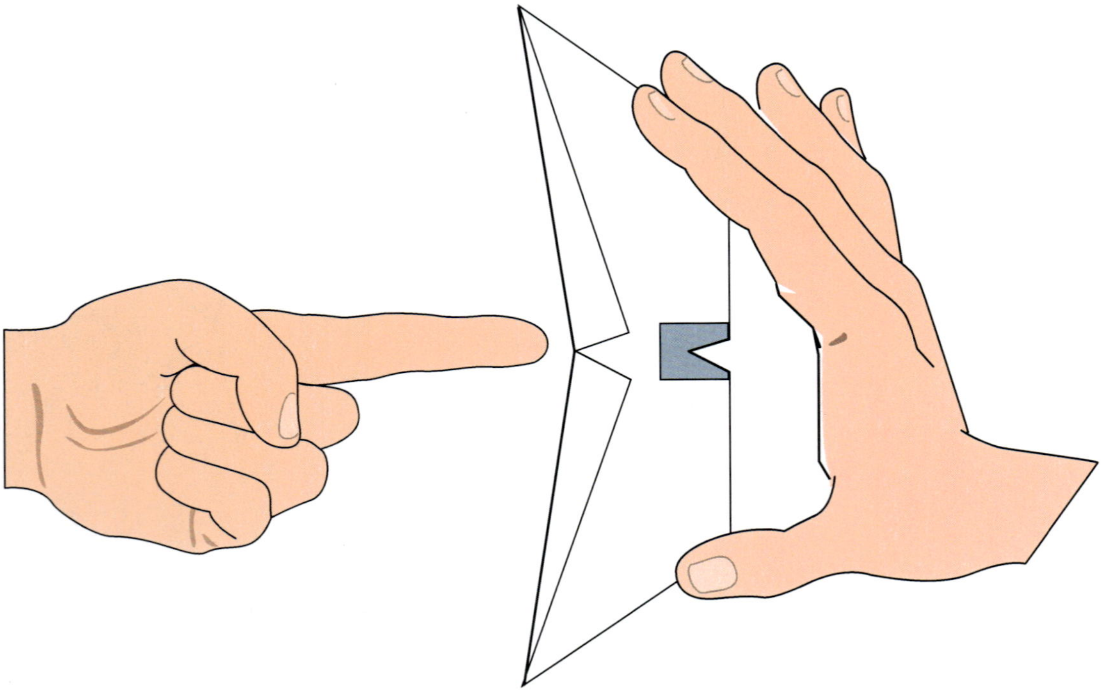

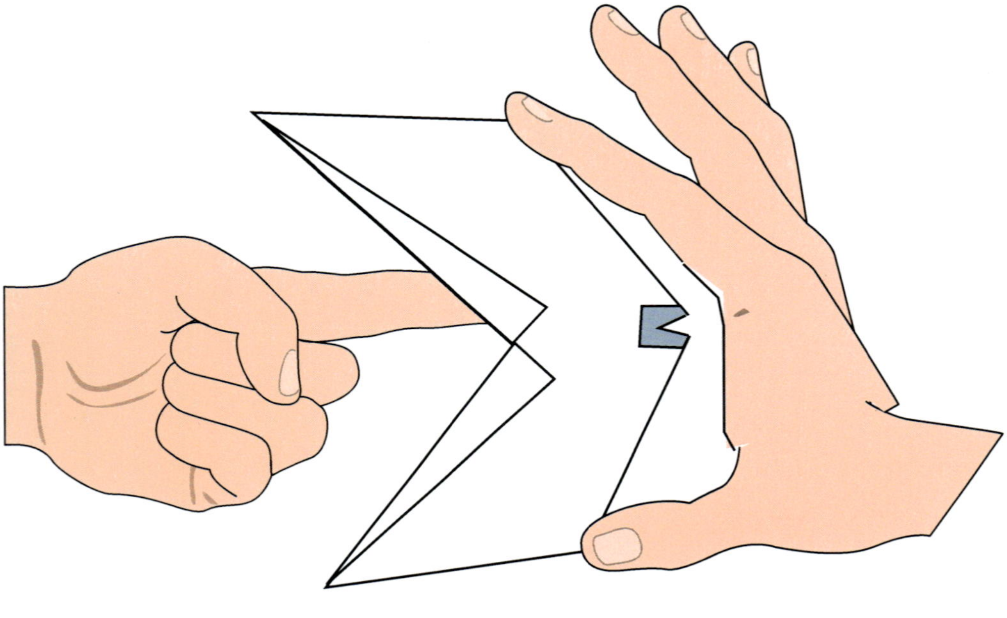

That looks easy.

To make the fish you need the same folds repeated three times (2 heads and a tail)

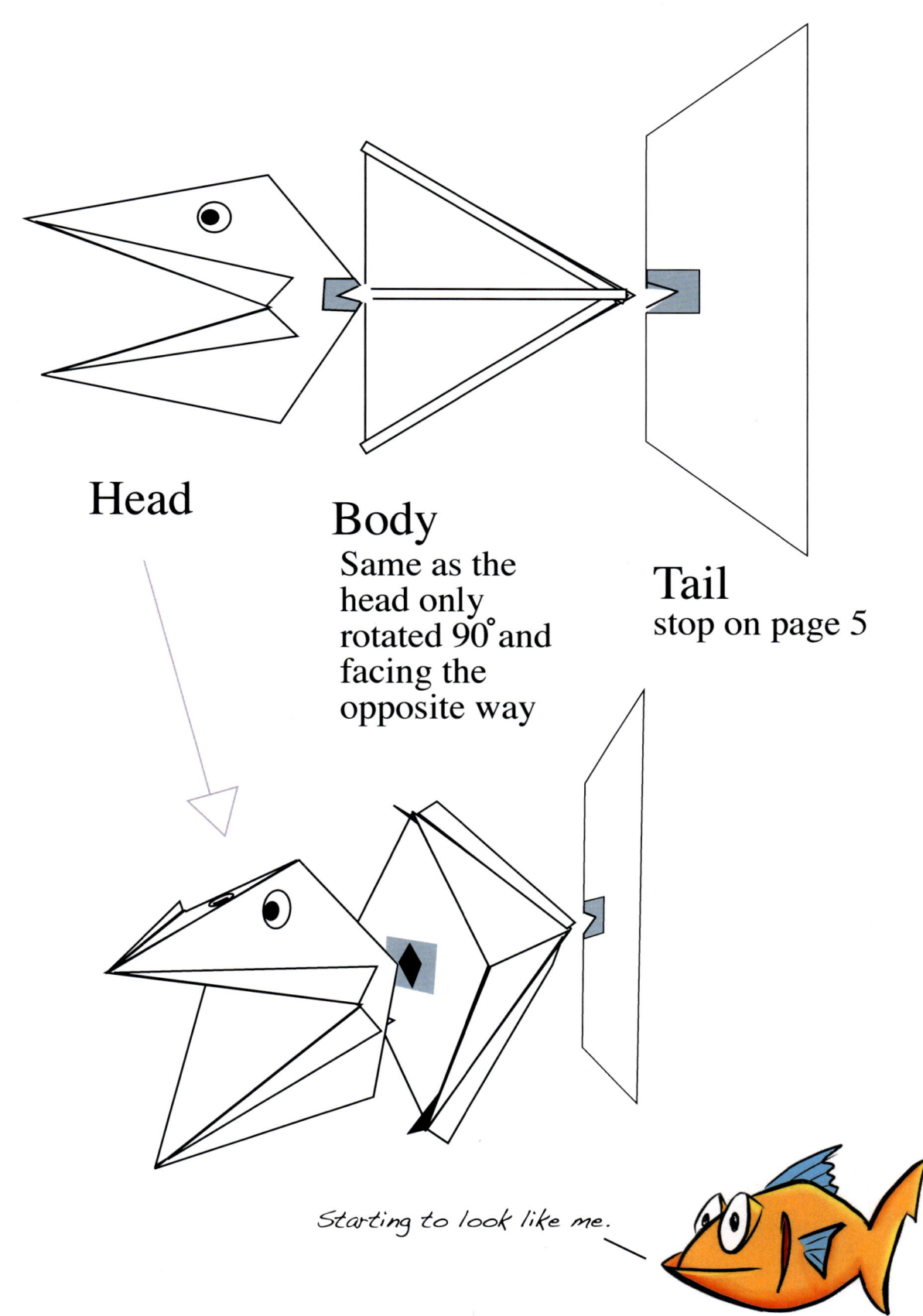

Head

Body
Same as the
head only
rotated 90° and
facing the
opposite way

Tail
stop on page 5

Starting to look like me.

Now comes the string, which makes our fish talk. Place a piece of tape on each end of the string and wrap it like the end of a shoelace. This gives more surface area when you tape it in the mouth.

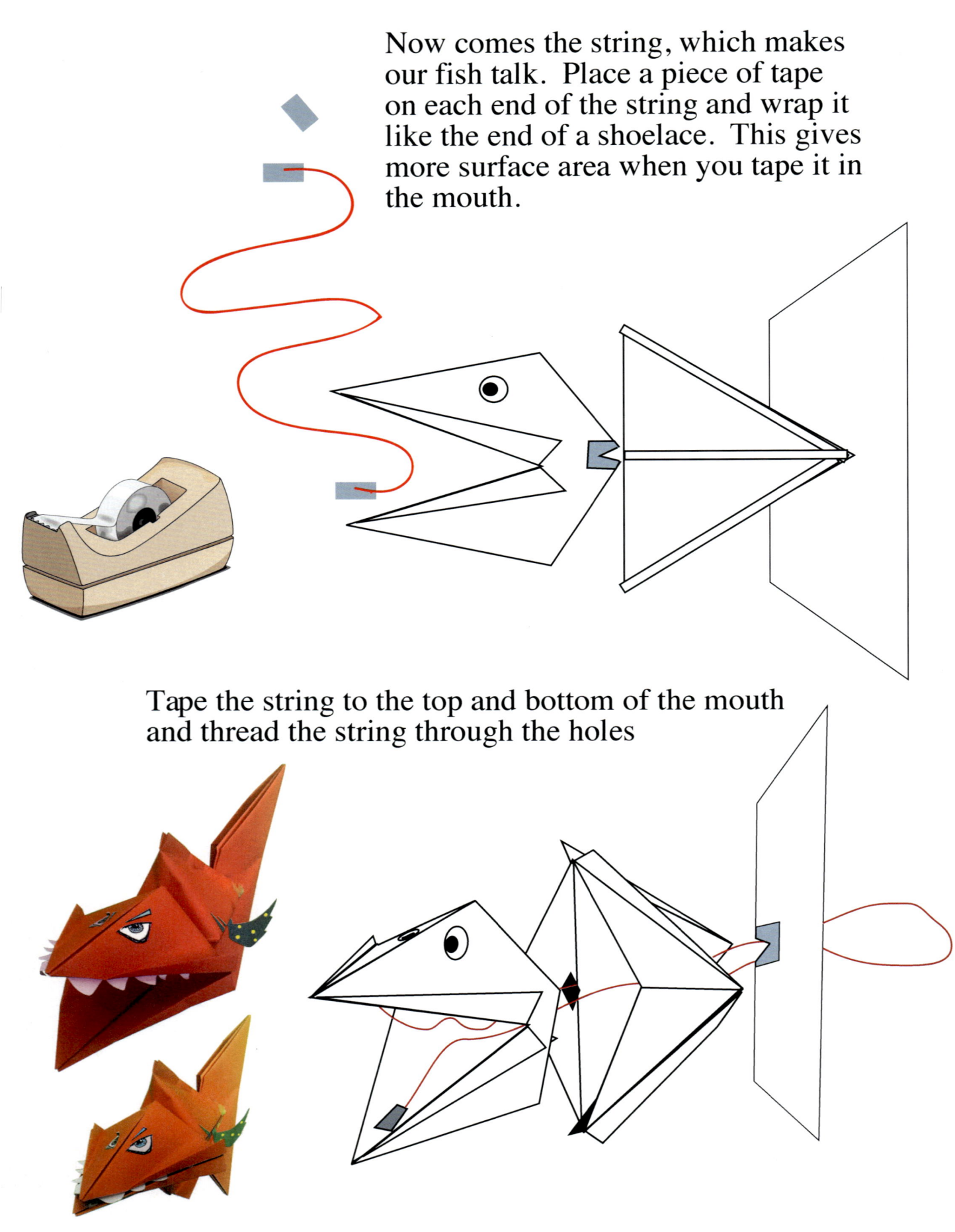

Tape the string to the top and bottom of the mouth and thread the string through the holes

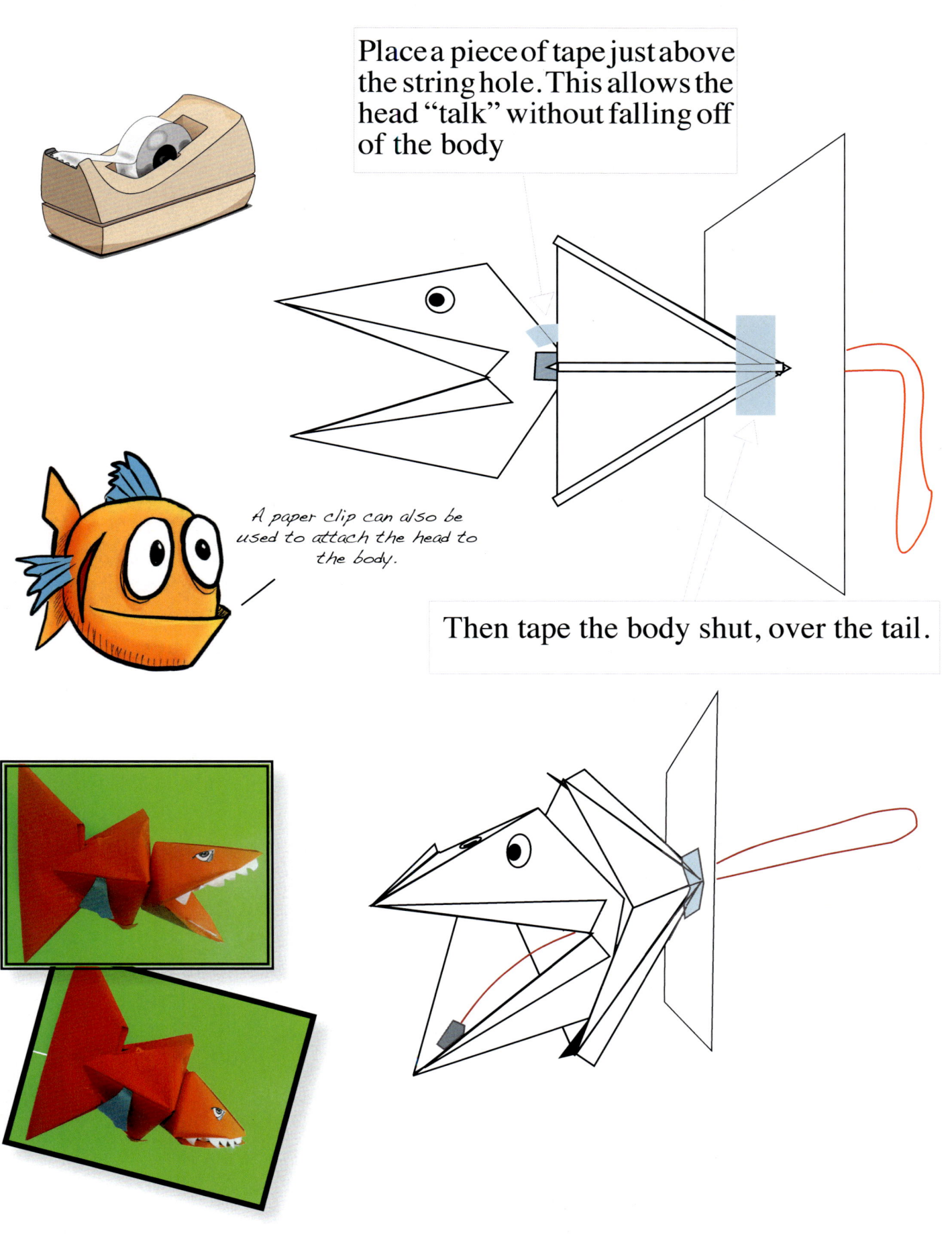

Place a piece of tape just above the string hole. This allows the head "talk" without falling off of the body

A paper clip can also be used to attach the head to the body.

Then tape the body shut, over the tail.

To Decorate your fish, you can use colored paper and any other materials. The back of this book has "templates" you can cut out and glue to your fish for eyes, gills and fins.

You can also download and print designs from **FOLDFISH.COM**
If you print on sticker paper they become "stickers".

Don't be afraid to invent your own designs.

Eyes
(happy or tough)

Gills

Fins

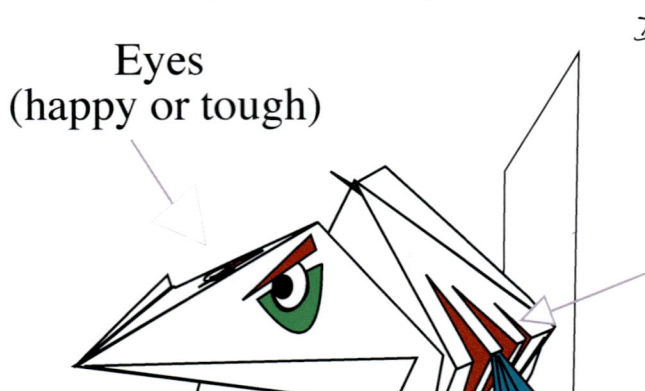

Fins can be made with cut paper, feathers or a sticker. Just place the end of the "fin" inside the fold on the side of the fish.

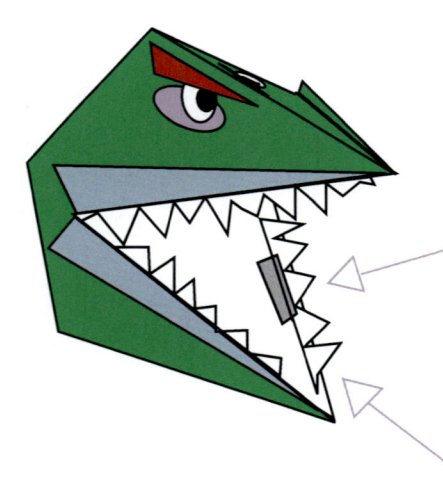

Teeth

To make a truly tough looking fish you need to add teeth. Just cut a strip of paper with one edge full of jagged teeth and tape or glue inside the mouth.

Cut and glue inside mouth.

THE CAPTAIN'S TALE!

THIS IS A STORY ABOUT A TREASURE SEEKING CAPTAIN, WHO MEETS HIS FATE ON THE HIGH SEAS.

When performing this story, make the folds and tell the story the way it was written. This will help you remember what fold to do next.

Be sure to take your time and build the suspense. Everybody likes a well told, exciting story. You can even use the fish to tell the story, while a partner performs the folds

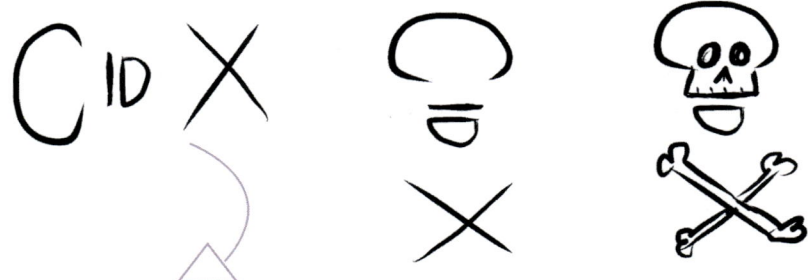

If you write the letters CIDX and rotate, you too can make a cool skull.

THERE ONCE WAS A CAPTAIN, WHO PUT ON HIS HAT EVERY TIME HE WENT OUT TO SEA.

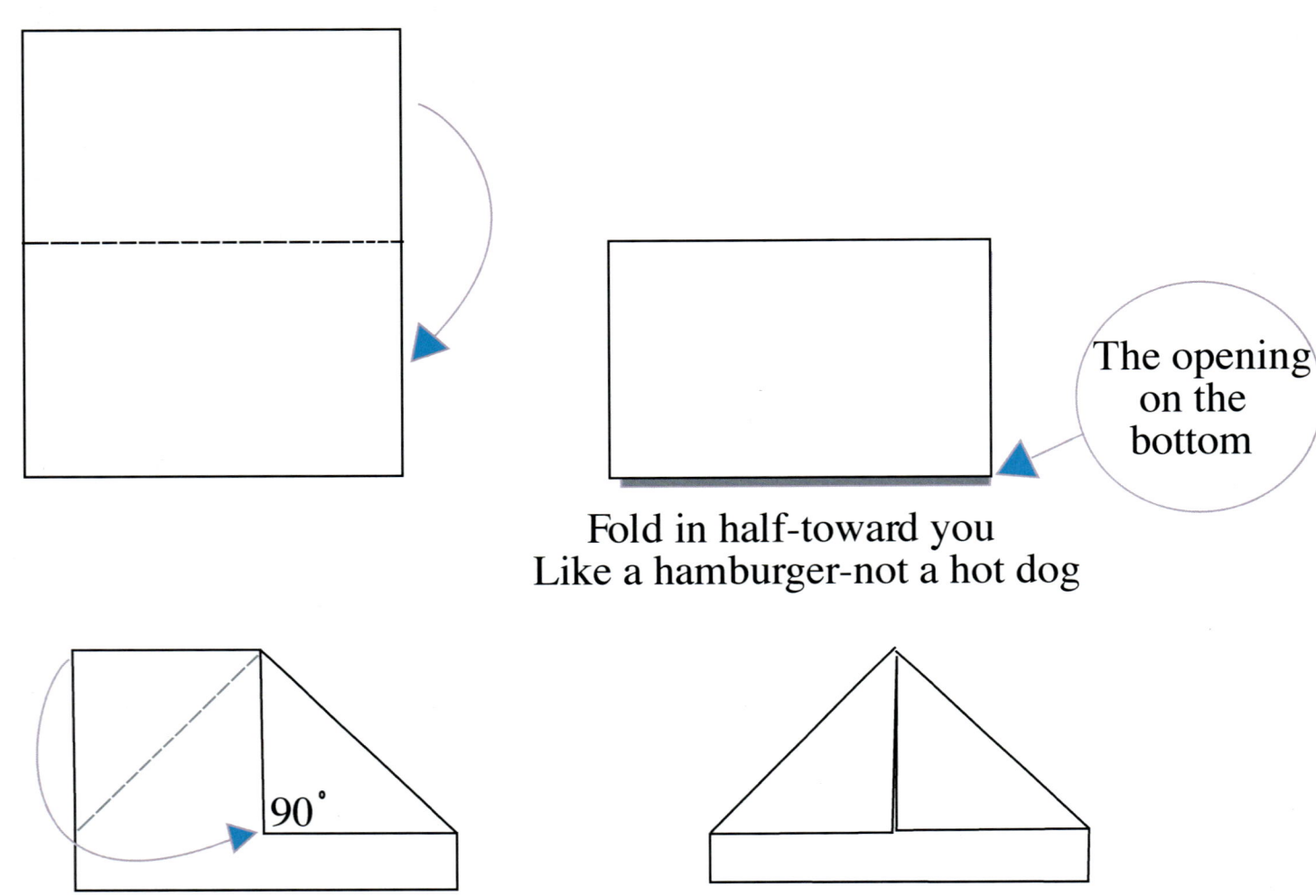

Fold in half-toward you
Like a hamburger-not a hot dog

The opening on the bottom

90°

Fold the corners down at 90° from the center
(like a paper airplane)

Now you need to create the brim of the hat for both sides

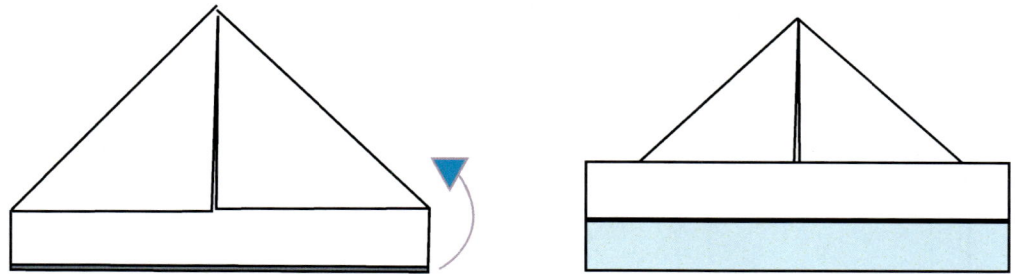

Fold 1 edge up to create brim

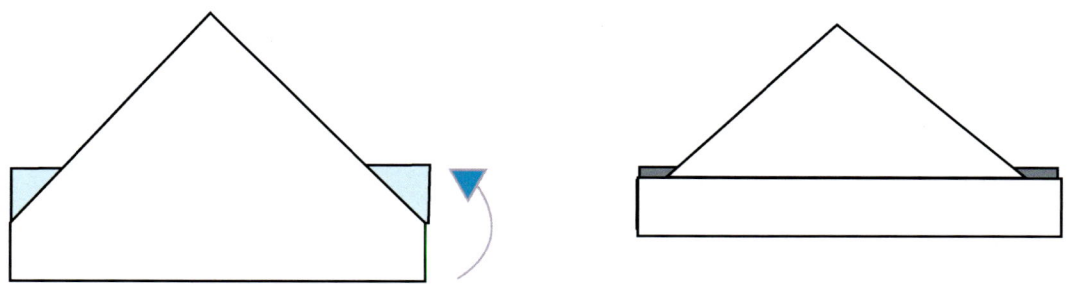

Flip over and repeat

You can now draw the pirate symbol, on the hat

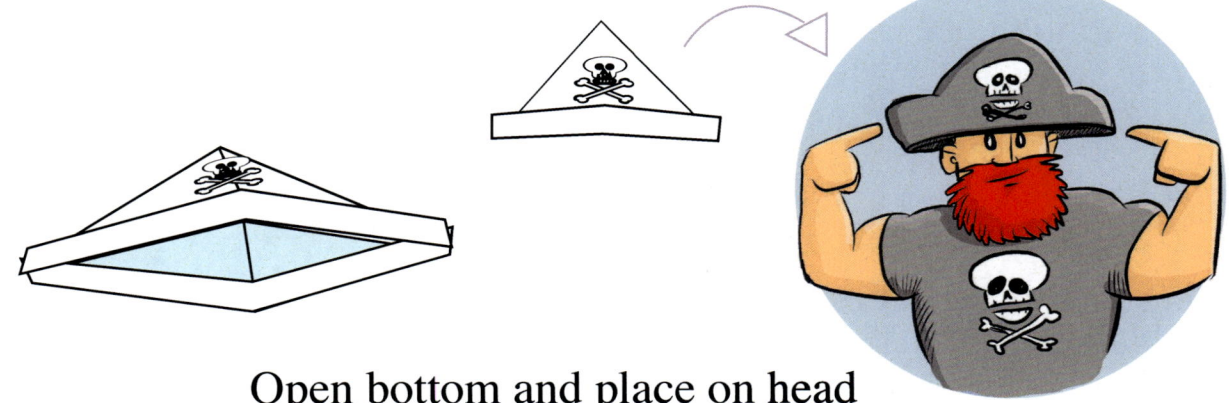

Open bottom and place on head

HE WOULD GO OUT TO SEA EVERY DAY AND LOOK FOR **DIAMONDS**.

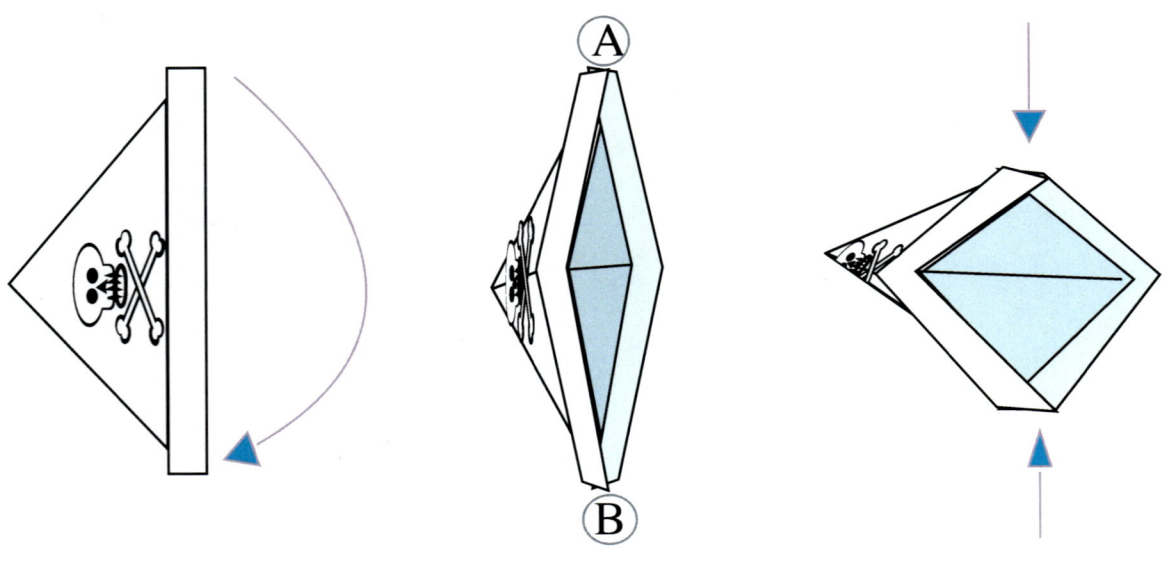

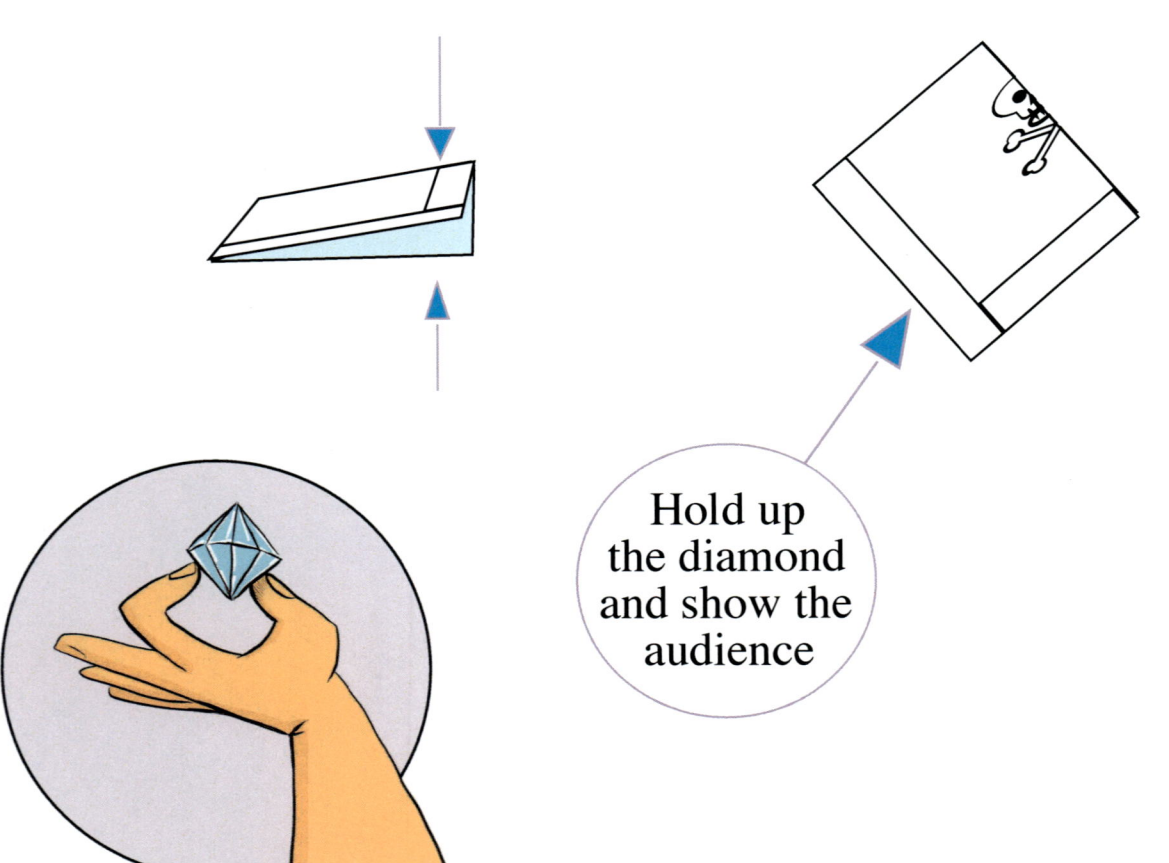

Hold up the diamond and show the audience

THE PEOPLE OF THE TOWN SAID "CAPTAIN-CAPTAIN...DON'T GO OUT, THERE IS A STORM COMING!"

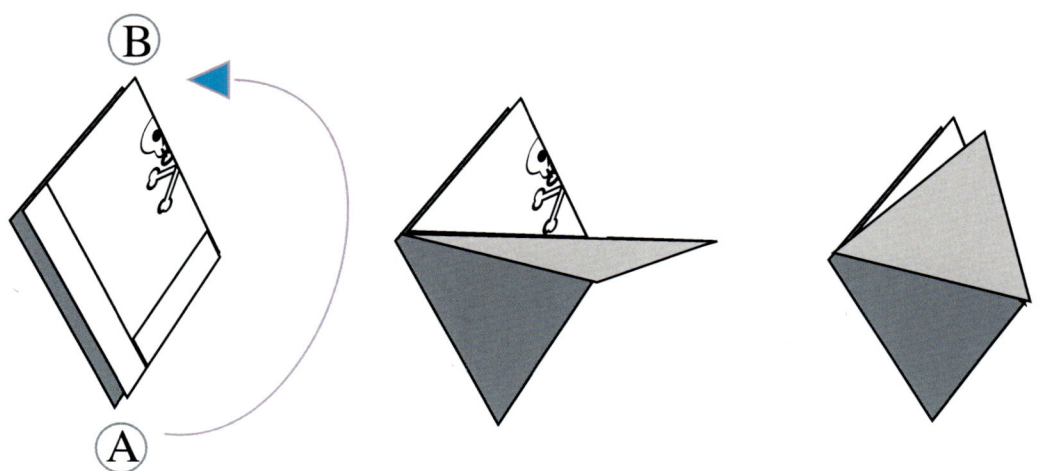

To create the sail, just lift corner A to B in the
front and repeat in the back.
The triangle is your sail.

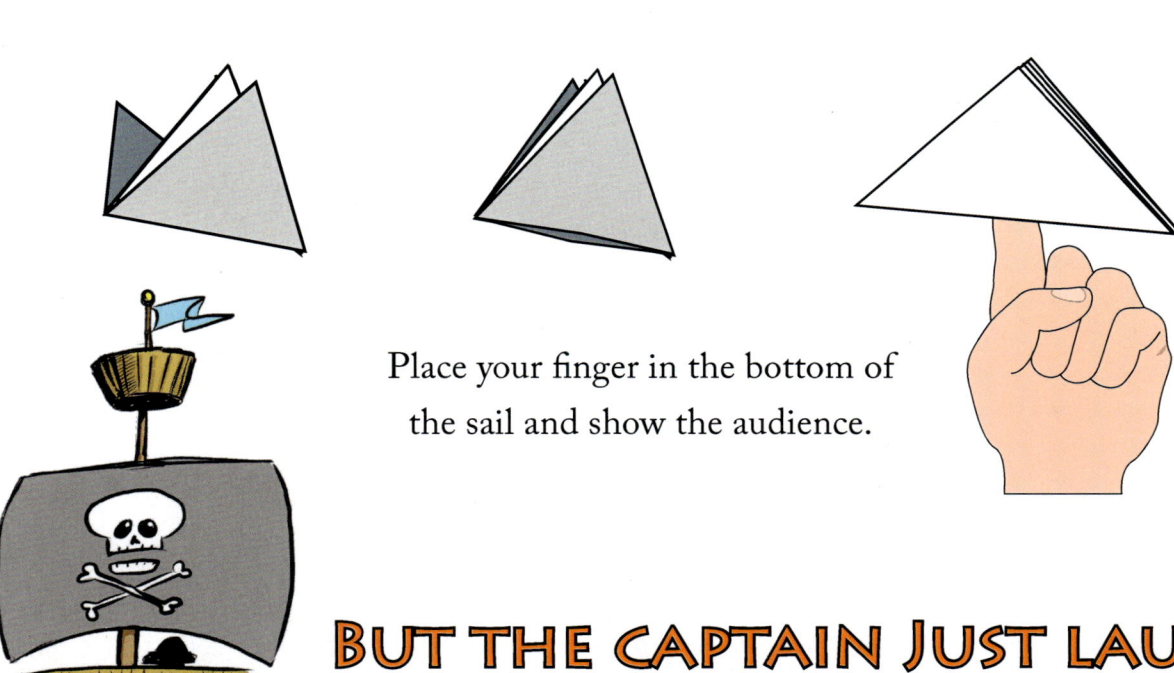

Place your finger in the bottom of
the sail and show the audience.

BUT THE CAPTAIN JUST LAUGHED "HAR HAR" AND SET HIS SAILS.

THE CAPTAIN WAS ONLY THINKING OF ...
DIAMONDS.

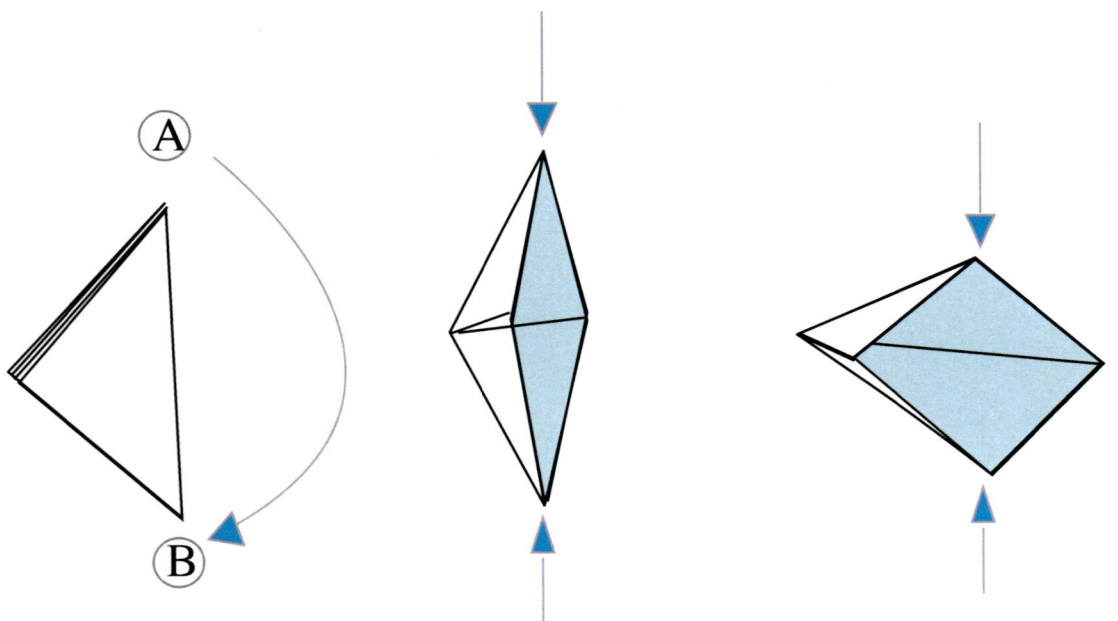

Now turn your hat sideways and push the ends
(A and B) together to create the diamond shape.

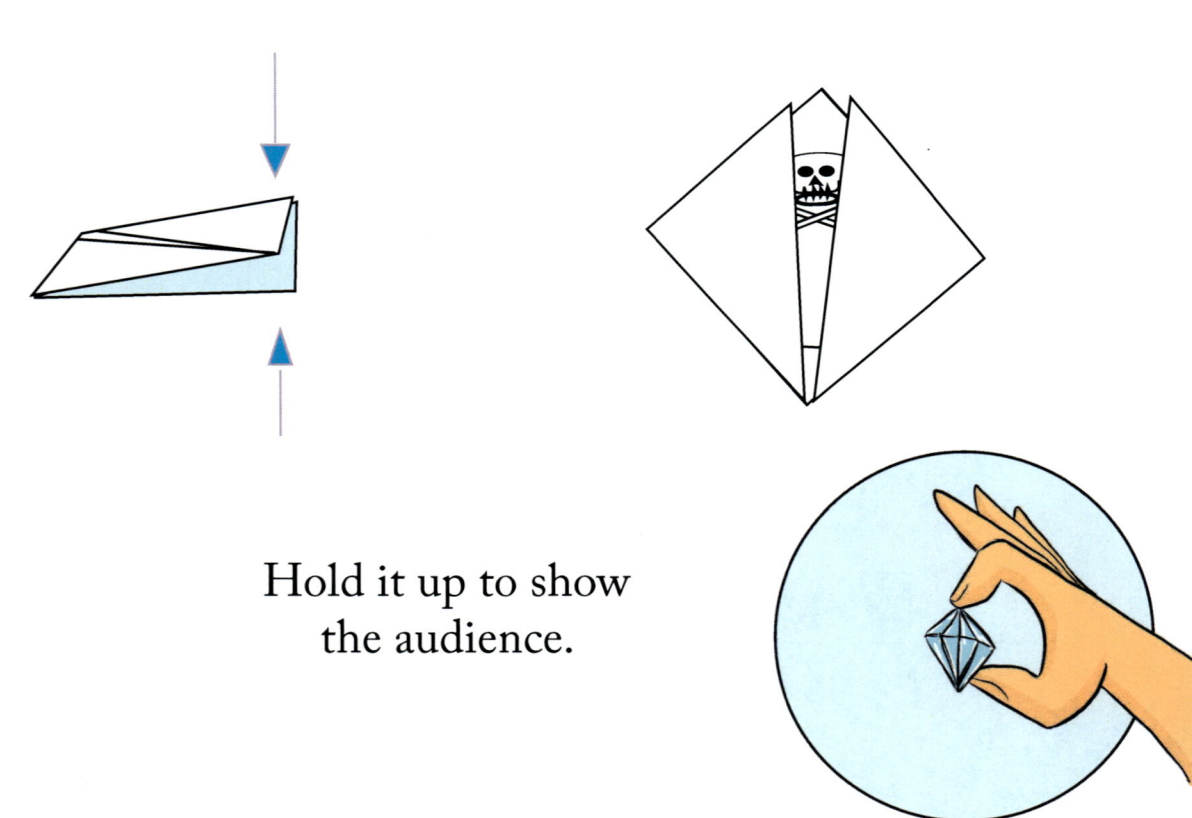

Hold it up to show
the audience.

SO THE CAPTAIN GOT INTO HIS BOAT, AND SET OFF IN SEARCH OF TREASURE.

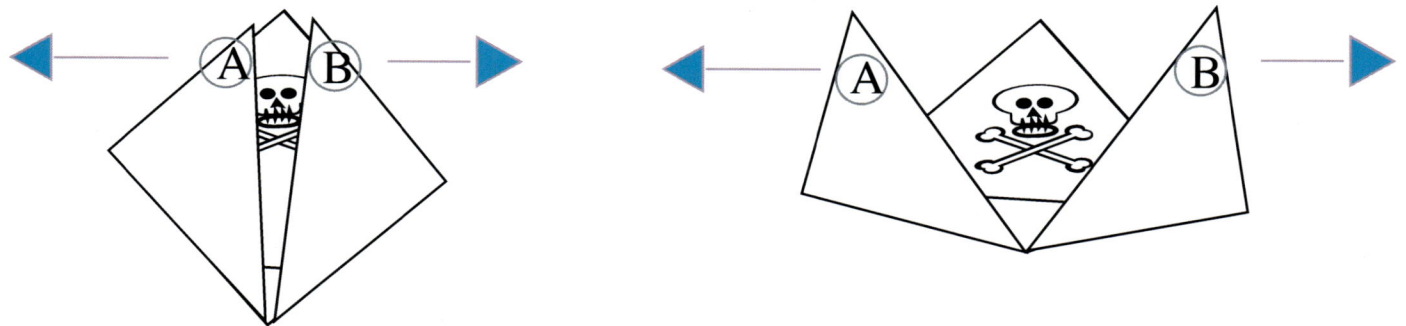

Now grasp A and B and pull apart in opposite directions

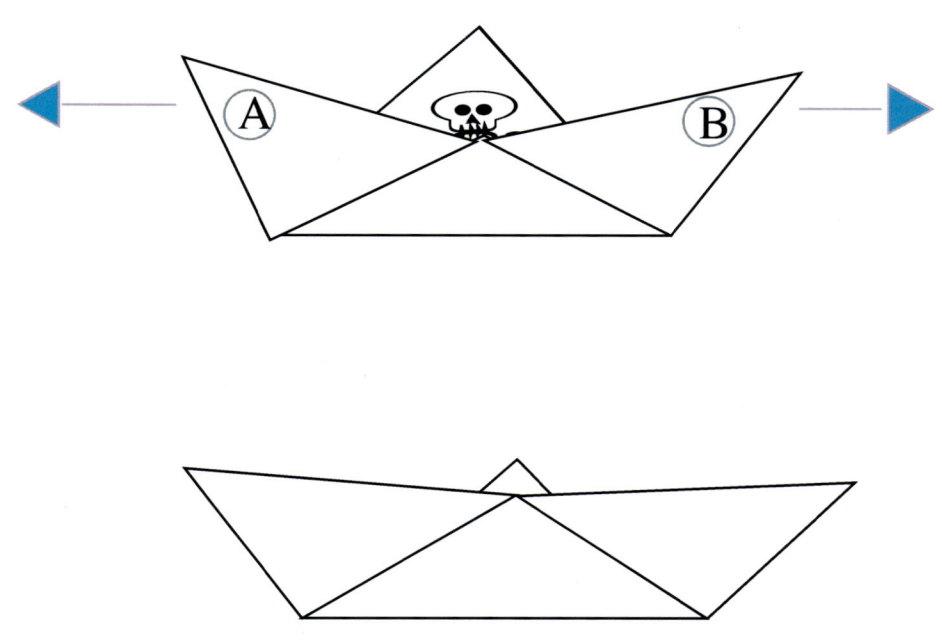

Trouble unfolding the BOAT?

Crease for easy opening.

If your boat doesn't smoothly unfold, then put A and B back to the diamond shape. Make another quick sail shape and then return it to the diamond. The extra fold will make it a smooth transition to the boat fold.

ONCE HE GOT OUT TO SEA, THE SKY GREW DARK AND THE SEAS WERE ROUGH.

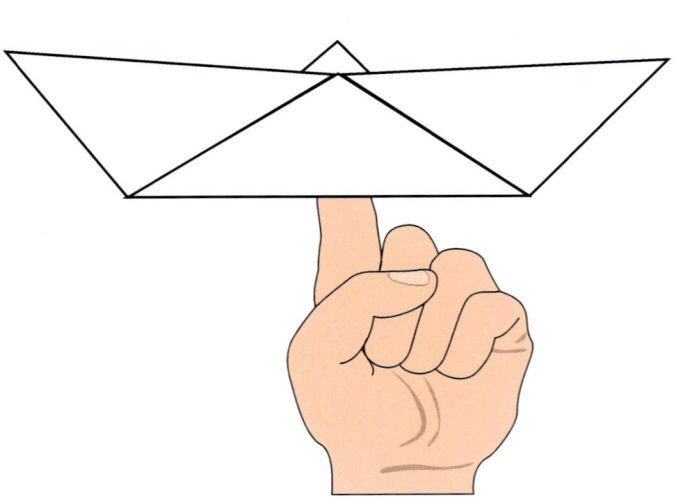

Wave the ship as if it were at sea.

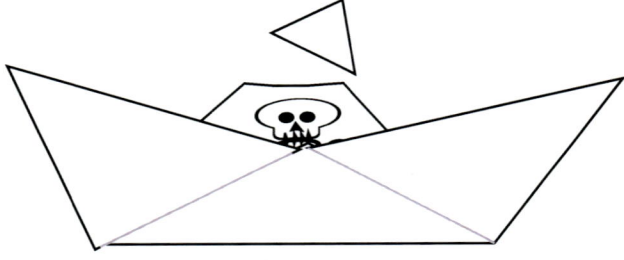

Now just tear as the illustrations show

SUDDENLY , A MIGHTY WIND RIPPED OFF THE SAIL!

A GIANT WAVE, RIPPED OFF, THE FRONT OF HIS BOAT.

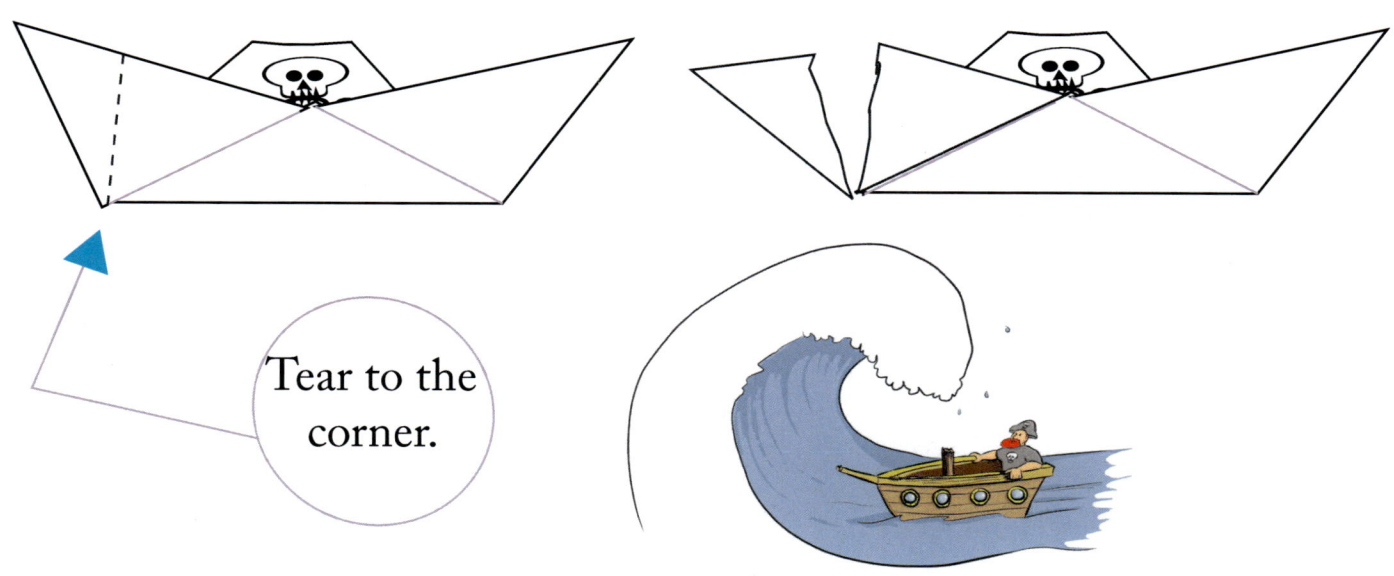

Tear to the corner.

THE CAPTAIN JUMPED TO THE BACK OF THE BOAT, AND TRIED TO RIDE IT LIKE A SURFBOARD... BUT IT WAS TOO LATE.

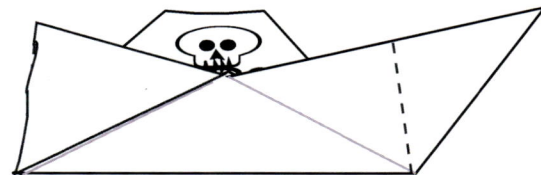
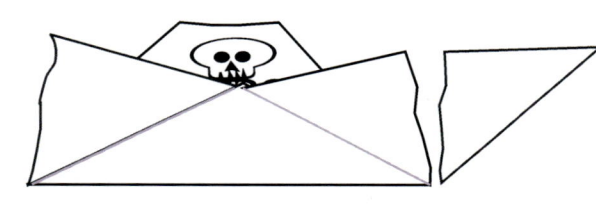

THE BIGGEST WAVE OF ALL, RIPPED OFF THE BACK OF HIS BOAT.

SOME PEOPLE SAY "HE MADE IT TO SHORE."

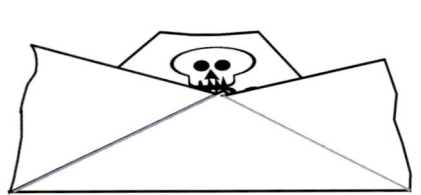

Unfold

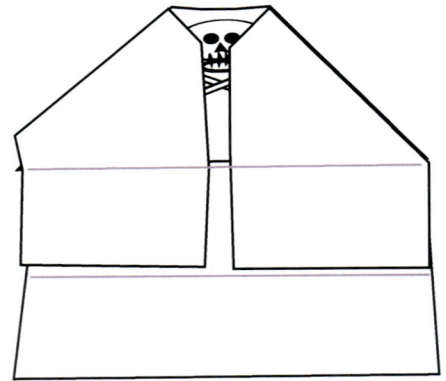

OTHERS SAY "HE WENT DOWN WITH HIS SHIP."

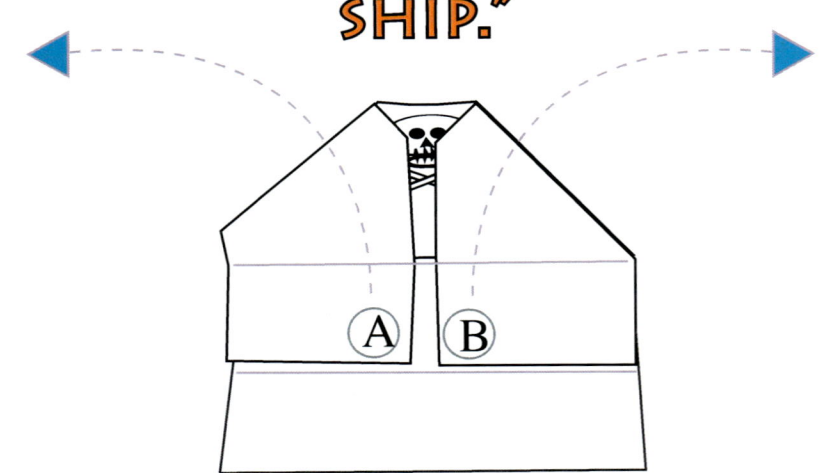

BUT ALL THAT WAS FOUND, WHEN THEY SEARCHED THE NEXT DAY...

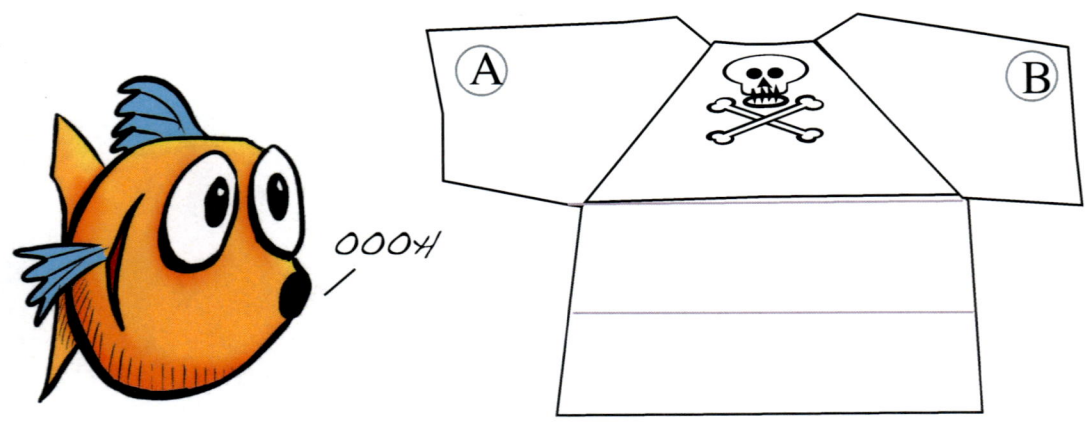

OOOH

... WAS THE **CAPTAINS SHIRT!**

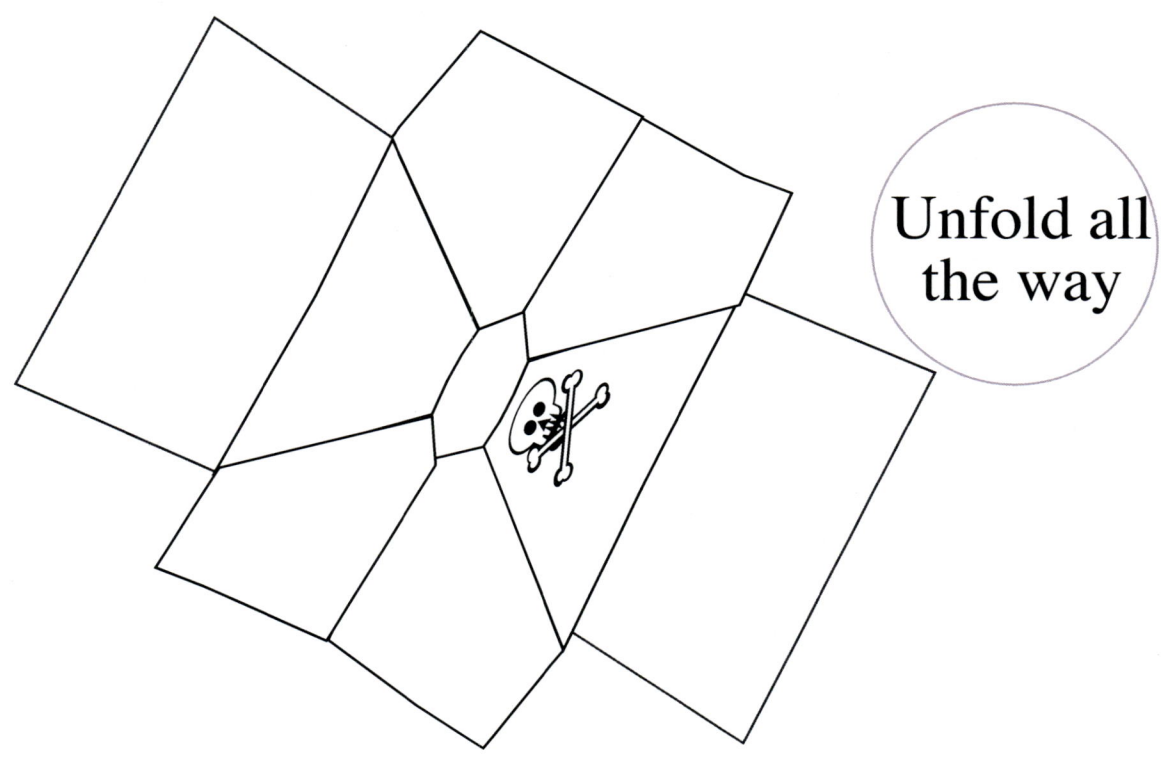

Unfold all the way

AND THEY NEVER FOUND THE "X" THAT MARKS THE SPOT WHERE HIS TREASURE LAY.

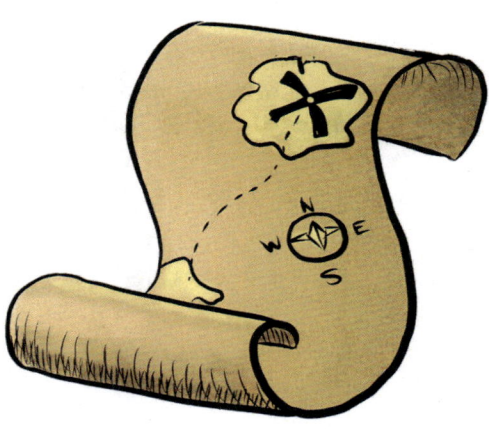

I saw the Captain on the island of Coronado, last week. He was surfing and living like a king.

Embellishments!
Make your own stickers

Here is where you can cut out and glue the "templates" to your fish. If you do not wish to cut up your sweet new book...Don't WORRY! Just go to foldfish.com and download the PDF's. Now you can print these on your home printer, anytime you want. If you print on sticker paper they become cool stickers. You also could just make your own designs, and maybe come up with something amazing!

Gills

These allow the fish to "breath" under water.

Cut them out and glue them to the side of your fish.

Fins

These stabilize and help the fish to swim.
Glue the small tab and slide into the crease in the side of your fish.

Eyes and Brows

Some eyes and brows are separated so you can change the looks.

Teeth

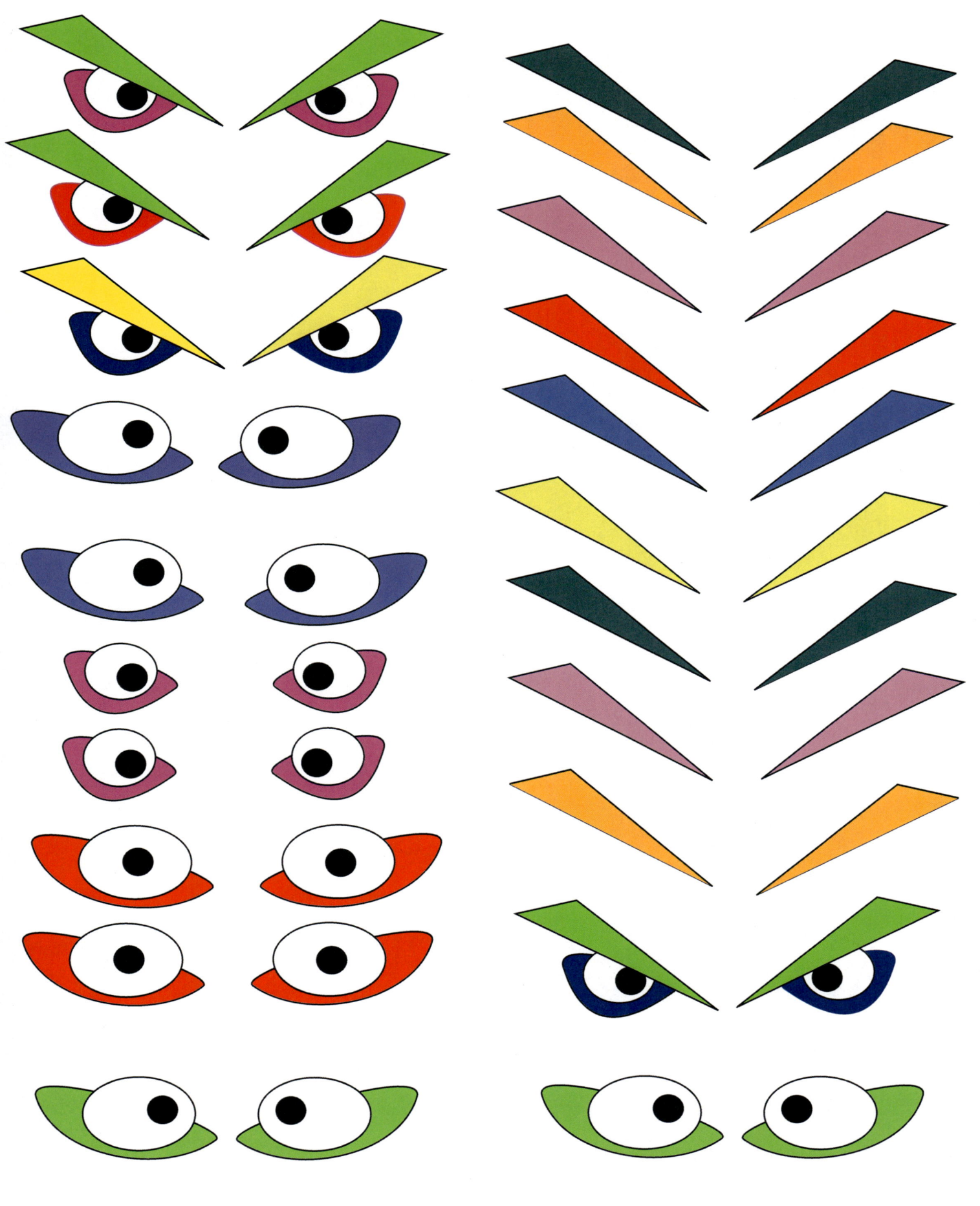

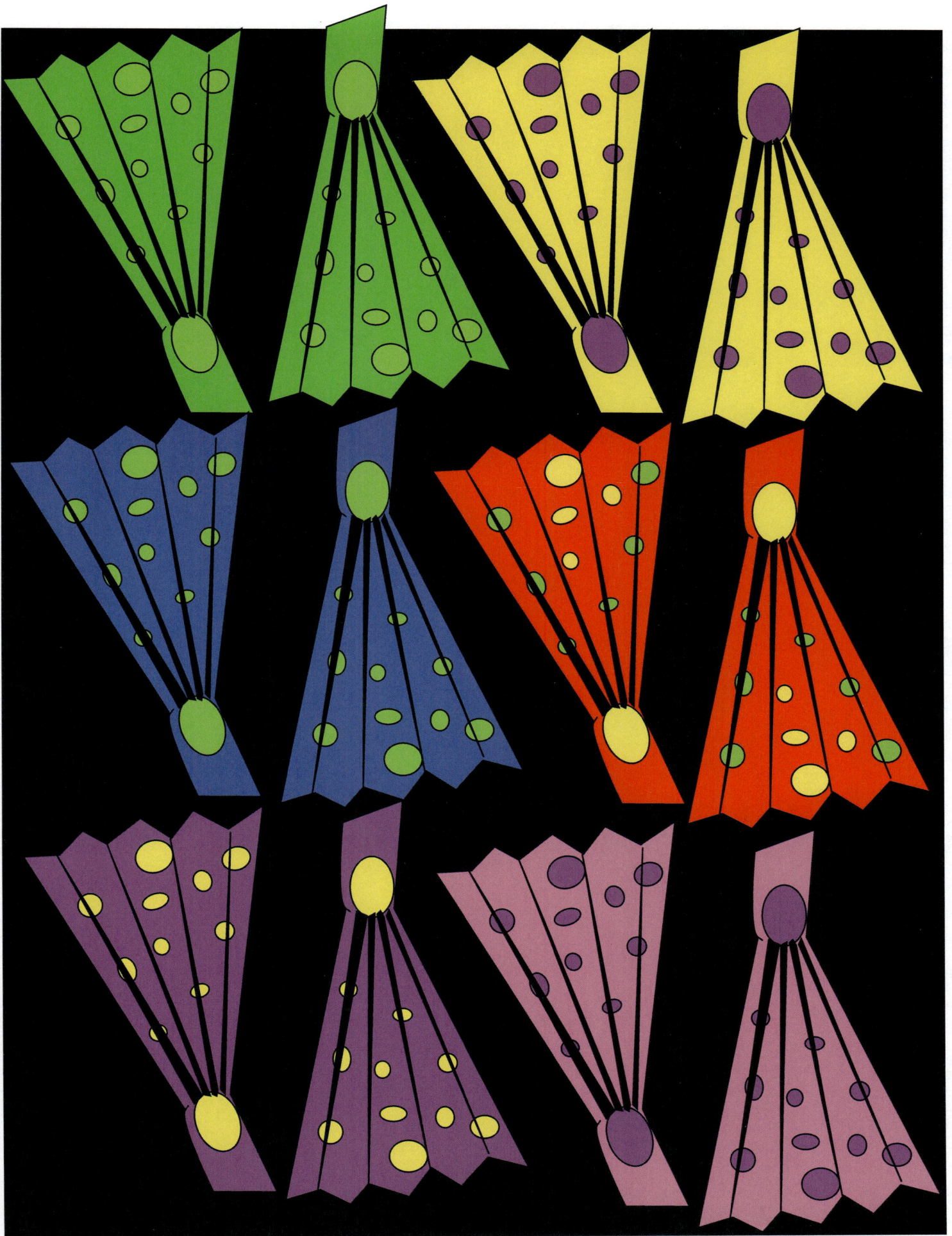

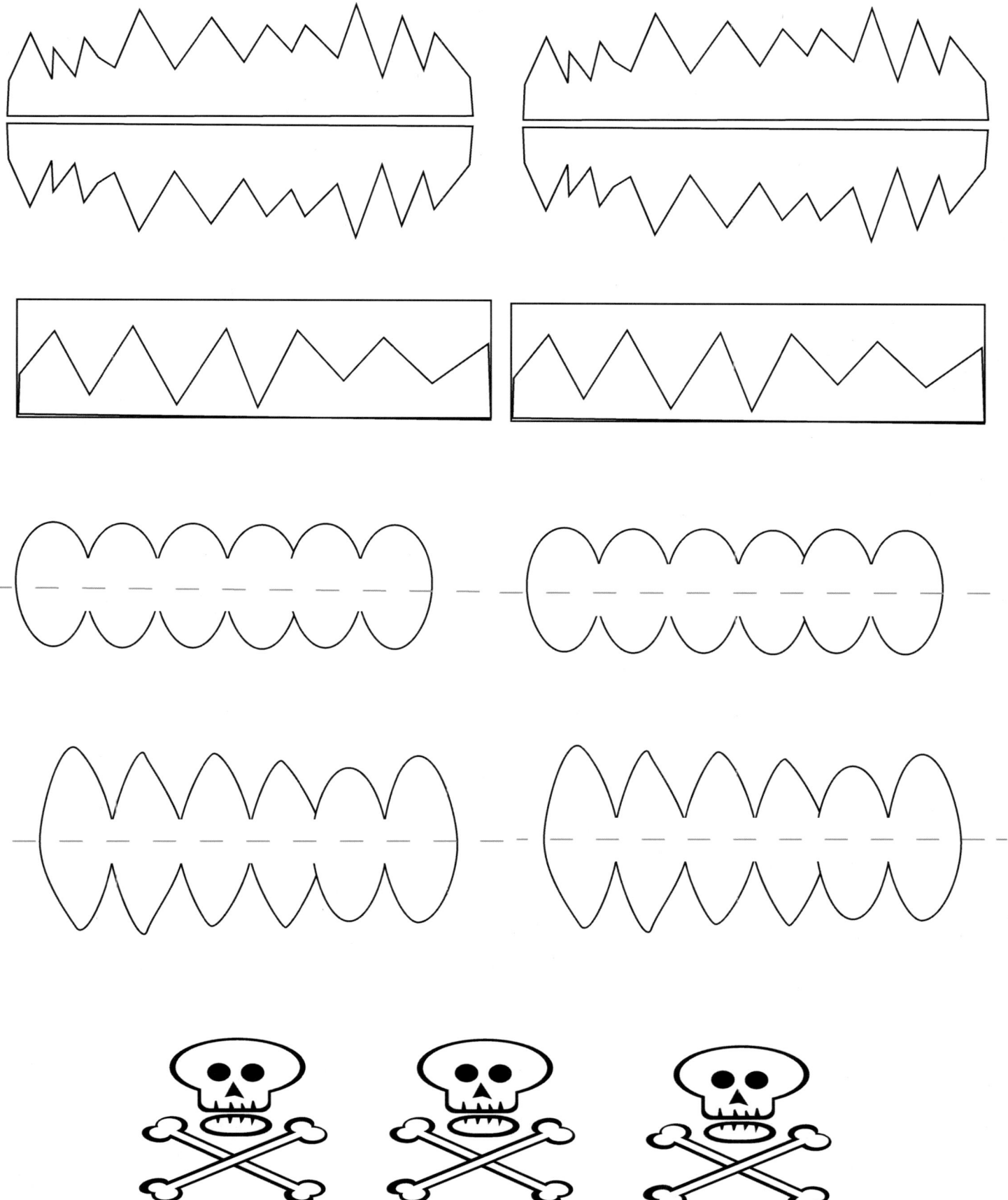

7 Things you have learned
from this book
(Without even Realizing it)

Following detailed Instructions
If you have completed a fish, then you have mastered complex directions.

Teaching Others
Break down big tasks into smaller steps.

Patience
It is easy to quit, but you kept going.

Geometry
Paper folding is a great way to learn angles and shapes.

Public Speaking
The #1 fear for adults doesn't scare you. You can now tell a great story.

Artistic creativity
You made your own decorations, and improved fine motor skills.

Problem solving
These fish are paper, so when they break, you are able to fix them.

All of these traits are synthesized when you create **new** animals and folds. To get you started I put some of my secret sketches on the next page. I gave very little instruction, so you will have to expand your creativity and problem solving ability. Have fun and keep folding

Thank you and **please** recommend this book to a friend.

SECRET SKETCHES

NOW THAT YOU HAVE SUCCESSFULLY MADE SOME FISH, I AM GOING TO SHARE SOME OF MY SPECIAL CREATIONS.

SCALE

TRY PLAYING WITH SIZE. SEE HOW SMALL, OR LARGE, YOU CAN MAKE A FISH. THE LARGE SCALE FISH USED COLORED POSTER PAPER AND STRONGER TAPE. I USED A PAPER CLIP TO ATTACH THE HEAVIER HEAD THE BODY. I ALSO USED PAPER CLIPS ON THE ENDS OF THE STRINGS, BEFORE I TAPED THEM INTO THE MOUTHS.

THE COUCH-NESS MONSTER

THIS PERISCOPE DESIGN IS PERFECT FOR PERFORMING A PLAY, FROM BEHIND THE COUCH. THE BIG MONSTER WAS MADE WITH A LARGE MAILING TUBE. THE SMALL MONSTER WAS MADE FROM A PAPER TOWEL TUBE. I CUT THE TUBE ON AN ANGLE, ROTATED IT, THEN TAPED IT BACK TOGETHER.

NOW ITS YOUR TURN TO DECORATE. REMEMBER, YOU CAN USE PAINT, PAPER OR WHATEVER YOU LIKE. GOOD LUCK AND USE YOUR IMAGINATION.

PAPER CLIPS

CUT AND ROTATE

STRONG TAPE

MAKE UP A COOL STORY.

Made in the USA
Middletown, DE
16 November 2016